Overheard by Conifers

Overheard by Conifers

John V. Hicks

Thistledown Press Ltd.

© John V. Hicks, 1996
All rights reserved

Canadian Cataloguing in Publication Data

Hicks, John V., 1907-

Overheard by conifers / by John V. Hicks. —

Poems.
ISBN: 1-895449-61-8

I. Title.

PR9199.3.H534084 1996   C811'.54   C96-920052-8
PS8515.I22084 1996

Book design by A.M. Forrie
Cover art by George Glenn
Set in 11 pt Goudy
by Thistledown Press

Printed and bound in Canada by
Veilleux Printing
Boucherville, Quebec

Thistledown Press Ltd.
633 Main Street
Saskatoon, Saskatchewan
S7H 0J8

Some of the poems herein have been published in *Ariel, Canadian Author, Grain,* and the *Prairie Journal of Canadian Literature.*

Thistledown Press acknowledges the support received for its publishing program from the Saskatchewan Arts Board and the Canada Council's Block Grants program.

CONTENTS

PICTURES AT AN EXHIBITION

FANTAISIE 9

APRIL LANDSCAPE 10

THE ROAD TO CANDLE LAKE 11

TEA-CUP AND DRAGON 12

THE WAY TO THE MOON 13

YELLOW MEADOW 14

THE PANS 15

SIPPING AT THE CUP OF THE MOON 16

FLAT WORLD 17

DAS LIED VON DER ERDE 18

LIGHT AND SHADOW

SEVEN RIVERS 19

WOODWINDS 20

HORN 21

LEGEND: THE STONES 22

SNAPPING BIRCH: AUTUMN 24

APPLE PICKER 25

EAR-RINGS 26

OVERHEARD BY CONIFERS 27

THE LATE SUMMER WEEDS 28

BERRY HARVEST 29

DRESDEN 30

LOST CITY 31

RATHER GO NOWHERE THAN A BOOK   32

TYKE TRYING ON DARK GLASSES   33

I PEN A FRAG MEANT IN DECIPHER   34

DISTORTIA   35

FIRST FALL   36

OVINALE   37

THE HOLY DOGS   38

FELIX   39

THE BLACK HOLE   40

OCCULTATION   41

OUTBURST   42

THE USES OF BEACHES   43

BACK OFF   44

SENTENCES   45

CERTAIN SYMPATHIES ARE EXPENDABLE   46

42ND STREET   47

AUTUMN NEARING   48

AUTOBIOGRAPHY   49

SNOW   50

EASTER   51

SCENE II   52

ANOTHER GROUNDHOG   54

I CAME TOO LATE   55

SOUND AN ALARM   56

MY BUTTERFLY   57

SAINT LEONARD   58

VERMEER: THE MILKMAID   59

SEVEN-PETALLED FLOWER   60

THE MUSHROOM MAN   61

SLEEP-OUT   62

NUDE WEARING HAT   63

CRITIQUES   64

MIST OVER DUBLIN   65

STITCHER'S MOON   66

PRIERE ZOOLOGIQUE   68

THE GONDOLIERS   69

A NEW COMMANDMENT   70

SET UPON BY DOGS   71

THE HIGH SEAS   72

SPIDERS   73

REVOLUTION   74

REFLECTIONS

LITTLE MOUSE   75

NIGHT VISIT   76

'LO, HOW A ROSE'   77

NATIVITY   78

FEAST OF THE TRANSFIGURATION   79

EMMAUS   80

I am back from the park.

FANTAISIE

Is it the artist's shadow
or the artist's dream

hovering there above the willows
drifting over the water

moving on the far shore
passing and returning

unsatisfied
restless as footsteps

Who engenders whom
of what is the making

one fashioning another
signature uncertain

APRIL LANDSCAPE

Who sat watching
waiting for
earth's unfolding

What directive did he
rise bend over to
inscribe

scan edit
hurry away
with

THE ROAD TO CANDLE LAKE

The quarter-hour
chimes softly
the grass has grown

the clock knows
no work is finished
the blade rises

the hand follows
the brush dries
soon soon

TEA-CUP AND DRAGON

Drink if you will;
my fire is in the cup.
Take, drink for good, for ill,
its contents up.

Think how a dragon's blood
spilled upon Siegfried's tongue;
how by its spell he heard
the forest bird
sing unwittingly of such a flood
of love as never sprung
out of the flaming pyre
of love's protecting fire.

Think upon love's reward;
how at a winter's breath
it countered the conquering sword
with the spear of death.

Drink if you will;
my fire is in the bowl.
Beware lest its fury spill
into the very soul.

THE WAY TO THE MOON

Do not listen for a footstep
behind you; keep no watch
for the rotted post,
the weathered word.
Let shadows show you the onward
thrust, scrunch of small stones
be your directionals. No one
treads else this course,
or will. If you would ask,

ask the lover at his tuning
of the suppliant lute,
the loved in her response to
all but inarticulate vows

(the frayed string,
the halting syllable.)

Replenish failing strengths in
each darkening phase. Assume
validity of the first premise,
hope of there being light and to spare
at the way's end.

YELLOW MEADOW

There you were in the yellow
meadow, a hand lifted,
outline of your face
moon-soft in gone-before-twilight
feature, a promise to reappear
in one dream or another.

I could have drawn your thought
spider-web across a green's growth
but for the bale wind
that rose to speak in the ear
of textures defiant of recording.

I turned from the yellow meadow
in a twilight's gathering,
in a dream's returning.

Night was a candle tipped
with your yellow flame.

THE PANS

What is in the sky —
formations, creatures, messages?
Earth accepts its apportioned light.

Hear the crusted sand
shattering wheel under.
A deception of bells.

Bells? Are the ages
ringing in sequence?
Time tolled eon by eon.

It is right that shadows dominate.
Kindle light, but let it keep
subservience here.

Is the hand here, or there,
that draws a straight line between us?
We cannot cross, nor they.

The storm filling the sky
is spirit. Be still. Listen.
Let it possess you. Consume you.

Never conflict but will
in time resolve.
The sand is at rest.

SIPPING AT THE CUP OF THE MOON

Darkness discloses you;
I see your form
outlined in black light.

The line's edge
shows you feature for feature;
I am not far from your presence

ever. Tilts in your hand
the cup. You drink ethereal light
that is one with darkness,

darkness of mind and memory
shrouding you as you stand
sipping at the cup of the moon.

Slivers of earthlight
give trial and fail
your earthly appearing.

I linger and know
what draught is taken,
what word not spoken.

FLAT WORLD

The little stones murmur one to another
how mighty we are. We have made light of curvatures,
the heresy of sphere. We have stricken down
the ships' masts rising from the sea.
We have defeated distance; now
the world's ends are known to us.

We have lashed the rod of power
across the sun. It moves to our will,
dragging stars and planets with it,
the moon and the courses of the moon.

We are a plain without end. We know
nor time nor season. Direction
maintains its clarities. All change
is stabilized.

            Come
into a land not backward drawn by shade,
not pitching forward into light.

Our pulse beats measures of the march.
We are the rhythm of the new beginning.
In the throb and rattle of our drumheads
                  long-necked creatures wait to be born.

DAS LIED VON DER ERDE

Beauty, conquering spirit,
the heart beats to
drums of your advancing armies.

Your stallion storm
pours over me, the thundering
of a thousand hooves.

The very earth, rallying,
rises to sing insistent
echoes of your battle-cry.

I am restless, without ease.
I cower under the making
of your terrible peace.

SEVEN RIVERS

Upside down the sky
would be layers of cake icing
thick cream the river
moving in chunk jellies
I am as young as gently
falling the autumn leaves
I am as old as frosted
the winter branches.

WOODWINDS

Earliest of all but one
of our lyric uses? Perhaps. Did Pan
begin it? Measurements between holes
were largely experimental. Even
the immortal ear, let us suppose, was
ill tuned at first. (There's comfort
there.) He hadn't the wit, though,
or attention span, to fix
reed into reed. Given time
he might have thought of it.
As it was, the hollowed tube
was plaintive enough. Any child
could have squawked a grass blade
for him, but he didn't ask.
Have we similarly divine
creations in us?

HORN

The moon is sharp tonight;
right, left, well may it stab
the unwary. Hand me
my fluttering cape. The arena
beckons. I must stand or fall
upon your challenge, upon
my moment of truth,
my deft and silvered sword.
Truth or fantasy,
one or the other.

LEGEND: THE STONES

She gave him back his pledge,
signature and all.
They lay at the sea's edge
at the night's fall.

The moon, when it rose,
full and empty and pale,
having spied on their repose,
heard a whispering gale

from distances unknown
begin to recount histories
that were their own;
begin to relate mysteries

of love and their own sense
of having not understood
love's dearth of recompense,
for evil, for good.

And when the shadow ship
that would bear them away
from night and the sea's lip
to a sunscorched day

beached, and bid them board,
they willed instead to stay
and become two stones, stored
in eternity's play

of waves and washing sands
and sighing of wind
and the wasting of love's demands,
kind or unkind;

each in dispassionate stone,
the spirit's turmoil ceased,
kissed by the sea alone,
imprisoned, released.

SNAPPING BIRCH: AUTUMN

I tell you this backdrop of gold,
hanging breathless from my October tree,
cannot display the perfection
it knew when, a surrounding flame,
it lit with its native profusion
eyes, hair, the smile's challenge
you offered, there in the long-ago
of your posing, light of your presence
blazing even now in memory.

I think I shall retain
this innocent roll with its missing
component, intact in its dark exposure,
and indulge the fancy that you may be
there again, waiting in the depth
of your silence
to enliven the processed print.

APPLE PICKER

Love's apples dangling from her wrist,
a prize of pickings, plump, red,
bruise not at all against the thumping
thigh. Thwarted birds sing sharp-beak
requiems from their summer choirs
and cool leaf aprons. What is food
compared to her songs of victories?

Go away, old woman with your patent
parer, competent to skin in sweeps
the succulent flesh. Core's coat of juice
will sicken in sunlight that retreats
before the advancing dial's
shadow. There will be time to
taste. Wait, wait, I tell you.

EAR-RINGS

Dogs dangling at your ears
warn me away.
I wouldn't want to be attacked
by lobes that were made
for nibbling, savaged
at the very gateway of my
tenderest petitions.
I'd rather endure fangs
of your own slashing,
sense you paddling rivers
of my surging blood,
poking in at landing places,
claiming right of discovery,
setting up defences,
waiting to be outnumbered,
facing a final onslaught,
surrendering only a step
this side destruction.

OVERHEARD BY CONIFERS

I fear to speak, fear
to whisper, fear even
indiscriminate thought. Who knows
the intent of trees? Those trunks
are sounding boards; those coned branches
garners of indelicate betrayals.
Needles do not fall until
each one has spent its sensitivity
on catching and recording
the least unguarded breath, the faintest
of admissions.

A forest is a fearful place
for children bred on carnivores,
witches, apparently abandoned huts;
a place to be avoided by
the child grown old who has retained
his earliest fears. Let me speak
on the open plain, the innocent expanse
of prairie, where nothing but impartial grass
listens. Those towering ones
would at a wink close in,
bend every ear, destroy me.

THE LATE SUMMER WEEDS

Cool in the slant of sun, the garden
entertains here and there a late
visitor. Controls are done with,
days of toil diminish. These few
linger informal in the freshening
air, unthreatened, as after contentions
the playing field rests empty, loiterers
idling, cheering a faded echo.

Summer is threadbare. Even the light
is late. There were voices, and these
have dropped to a whisper of occasional
chirrups, part memory of nestings, part
projections into a long journey,
creative urgencies at rest,
acceptance of a season's ending,
gains forgotten, small losses untallied.

The heart too is still. Surges, strains,
pressings to victories, all softened now.
There is time for reflection, time
to refrain from determinations,
time to accept the sanctity
of silence, prepare in its depths
the entertainment of the new chilling
airs, the drawing in of darkness.

BERRY HARVEST

We came with strawberries from the woods,
woods merry with laughter,
our laughter, our small harvests
luscious in baskets.

We left our laughter in the woods,
we sat in sunlight tasting
tang and flow of our gathered
fruits, mouth to mouth flowing.

The distant woods will not forget
our laughter, nor will the bright-eyed
birds, picking here and there
at spilled berries, our berries,

our innocent harvests, our
memories of sun and singing
wind, faintest echoes that remain
to bless them still, the silent woods.

DRESDEN

There was a horn in Dresden.
Utter the prairie wind.

Invoke the night sea
heavy with moonlight.
Who shall give words
to silence?

Mystic of instruments,
most of comfort, most
treachery of love,
the false hunt impending.

Watchwoman, wave
a warning shawl.

Impale upon the outspread arms.
Transfix with the blunted spear.
The clocks of Dresden
tolling their hundred hours.

LOST CITY

A cry came out of the lost city.
Find us, adventurers;
turn your steps to untried paths.
We are here. We wait your coming.
We starve; we languish. We are given
to dreams of rescue. Find us.

Find us, excavators. Buried
in silt and ashes, we are deprived
of breath and sensibility.
We recall threads of life
pulsing within us; we, long departed
layer under layer of history. Find us.

Find us, visionaries.
Follow movements of air,
slant rays of planets. Sense
the mystic in our imaginary
compasses. Follow our needles.
There; go there. Find us.

Find us out, innovators.
All we had invented
rusts in our streets. More
than the keenest mind imagined lies
stacked in our storehouses.
Find us. Make us again.

RATHER GO NOWHERE THAN A BOOK

A log to sit on.
Small birds wide-eyed,
chirpless. An owl
over my shoulder.
I don't know why wisdom
kibitzes, let alone
why blinding daylight
undoes its rest. Everything
I don't know companies
me in this wood.
A thread of hawk-cry
tells me my book is riveted
far away,
far up there where
the pinpoint eye
perceives us, me and
my book. This library
of trees, scuttling creatures,
earth probings, eschews
the sanctity of clouds,
accepts me,
approves my learning and
my leaping bonfire of
silence.
Rather go anywhere than without
my book.

TYKE TRYING ON DARK GLASSES

Owl sees like this
sees me in the
dark sees
frog jump
big eyes like
baseballs I'm a
blue fly I'm
a crockledile
you can't see me
can you I'm
a big green turtle
aren't I

I PEN A FRAG MEANT IN DECIPHER
for Gerry Shikatani

Whirr are you gong
singing presses
your print song
your speech excesses

wider than birds
your where range
definitive words
impervious change

ask me away
never to come
lips astray
nerve numb

tell me young
tell me old
myself have sung
diffident bold

channel or shelf
I you
to a like self
true true

DISTORTIA

for Gerry Shikatani

Ears ex/dis tended
as visual hysteria
invite one to listen
inattentive. What you intercept
is counterchoice; by hazard-hap.

Someone racing through
the house
slamming paper doors.
Eardrums aquiver
crash by recycle crash.

Futures already forgotten;
memories project,
overtake them.
Why will that spinning wheel
not sense me alone?

FIRST FALL

The first river did not know
where to go

had not venture to construe
what to do

left largely to meander
discover the sense of *wander*

nosing around rock and boulder
while the world grew older and older

hardly a hand for guiding
its seaward sliding

suddenly a great push
a bid to gather and rush

over an edge and become at all
the first waterfall

thrilling to the close embrace
of infinite space

ever to remember the ecstasy
of being for one plunging moment free

reckless in which it must have revelled
like a beautiful woman
with
her
hair
dishevelled

OVINALE
for a CBC cartoonist

Sheep dancing to
shepherd's pipe

under carved
moon in course

two by two
snuggled fleece to fleece

bodies folded
breast to breast

Stones on outcrop
cultivate silence

moon sentrying
shift your gaze

emptied cotes
prepare couches

Whose is the song
sheep or shepherd

whose the longing
animal or man

ask ask
clicking feet

answer
ogling stars

THE HOLY DOGS

A dean's dog
A curate's dog

They prowl the crypt,
poke into kitchenette and cupboard,
patter about, sniffing down
morsel and crumb left lying
on neglected floors;
innocent, unwary save for
the ready bark challenging distant
footstep or slamming door;
sentinels of sorts, jealous
guardians of ferial silence.

Lord, protector of all things,
withold judgement, keep them
from fear's intrusion,
from brute defilements;
look upon them,
favour them,
let it be meet that we meet them
on holy ground.

FELIX

A bishop's cat

Cats should curl
up. This one, on a whim,
rolls ungainly over,
spine swayed, legs and paws
extended, reaching out
as though to invite and embrace
something lingering just beyond
reasonable conjecture.

                            Felix,
by turns companion,
pacifist, killer,
what might these spirit speculations
be? Dare one inquire? We, smug,
from upper-end-of-scale assurance
look down with traces of
ill-advised derision.
A safer stance by far
to admit our sensual limitations,
to concede there are things it were wiser
never to question,
never to be known.

THE BLACK HOLE

She came to me out of a black sky and her head crowned with a sprinkle of stars. Her hair flowed in astral light. She touched me, and I fell into deep certainty of sleep, and dreamed there. All the armament of heaven thundered. The drums of my ears joined the tumult. The constellations whirled about. The zodiac ring closed in. I spoke with the bear, the archer and the bull. The fishes swam against my eyes. Black is total absorption. There is full absense of light. Deepen. Deepen. Only voices now. Despair of being sucked into darkness. There is no earth. Earth is a failed memory. What was the substance of love? Will you dance with me? I had never danced in darkness, but the voice was sweet. My arms folded about nothing so lavish ever. I am in the present again. There is no past. I wish no future. A warmth, a blood warmth, enveloping me. A transmission. It begins in the arms and encompasses the whole. There are simple words I can no longer pronounce. My mind recounts them. Earth. Life. Waking. Sleeping. I cannot speak. The tongue rejects all muscular response. The tongue is captive. Pressed down. Absorbed as the body is absorbed. Words in the ear that fail all repeating. Now. Now.

OCCULTATION

The man in the moon
plunging down the sky
in his flying saucer
to enfold
Venus in his arms
one prisoned hour.

Will she reappear
blushing Mars-red, we wonder?

No need, pale disc, to divulge
celestial ecstasies.
See how we cast our shadow
upon your precincts.
We too are aware of privacies,
of impassioned hours.

OUTBURST

I shouted so loud at the moon
certain syllables came back to me
sprinkled like stars

the full of my outburst
escapes me but I think
your name was enphrased in it

I stand now
feeling flashes of its echo
falling about my shoulders

stinging my eyes as I wait
piecing together perhaps
an echo of you

all I shall ever know
letter by letter stabbing
at the memory's ear

THE USES OF BEACHES

Figures in beach hats
lumped on sands, poring over
shells and distances. Don't tell them
they should plunge in, immerse themselves,
refresh their bodies. Beaches are
for meditation. What they absorb
over and above the sun
will drain its way through the mind
and come out or
not come out
in memoranda to be put on file
in the universe. The recliners
are something other. Direct
your peremptories to them or to
the lovers whispering follies
on blankets, under umbrellas,
in your impatience to
get them into the sea.

BACK OFF

Just once I want to swing
in under the guard-rope, fix
the great glare with my lesser, say
beast, here we are, born
each into captivity, carrying
suppressed race angers, false
fronts of content, ready
at a flash to loose the spirit
for one more foray, bars
or no bars, make gestures
of ferocity, tear off an arm
here, a scalp there, be master in
the momentarily unconstricting cage.

Should I survive
to back off and consider, I shall have set
communications at rights, reached
a moment's understanding
between two worlds, two concepts
of survival, two meetings in the snarled
history of the cosmic mind.

SENTENCES

There is no stillness like
the stillness of flowers;
of no like silence do we learn
our accusations.
We stand assessed by
petal upon multicoloured
petal. We are judged
by juries boxed in sunlight.

We stand faint-heart, we turn
one by one away, our sentences
unspoken, our small guilts
bared in the true revealing
of all we have done, all
we have left undone.

CERTAIN SYMPATHIES ARE EXPENDABLE

Now, the clay-necked giraffe is nothing
if not fragile. In the tradition
of pigeons and churchwardens he
shatters easily.
                    (There — you've dropped it.
Poof — the buckshot runs it down
like stepping on an eggshell.
Puff — fragrance of Virginia
escapes the snapped conduit.)
                            Moreover,
in contemplation of imagined whiplash
one cannot but feel appreciative
of the fact that he, poor creature,
has so far been spared existence;
for even his admitted figmentation
scarcely stands off a twinge
of inductive agony.
                    One musters
gratitude for the smallest mercies,
notwithstanding in the gamut of compassion
certain sympathies are expendable.

42ND STREET

It is said elves live
in the old house on 42nd Street;
that they can be heard
chattering to each other
behind sagging-shuttered windows
in the very early morning, sometimes
late at night. One was observed
scrambling across the roof
by a girl who wore thick glasses.
Seeded honeysuckles in the cluttered yard
wave to them in windy September periods.
Once a porcupine, if you please,
trundled the half-rotted relic
of sidewalk up to the front door
and was not let in.
                      You will have heard
of staid office fathers, hands and knees,
playing make-believe horse, carrying
small children on their backs,
bucking bronco-like, unable
to throw them off; and mothers who
circulated deliberate literatures
subscribing to innocent deceptions
become fact; so you will know
there may indeed be elves living
together, a closed and secretive community, in
the old house on 42nd Street.

AUTUMN NEARING

We watch the light weakening
not day by day
but a selection of days,
portions of time falling back
where they belong. Summer was a visitation
replete with blossom and extemporaneous
lyric, the formal offering
of food from the earth as though
life were dependent upon life
to maintain semblance of activity
season by season. It is so,
and we forget in the solemnities
that there is a time for returning home.
Our home is winter, winter and its
gift of silence. Small wonder white
is accepted in the heart as purity. Still,
there is one more song to sing
before the birds leave us, before boats
moor and we scuff together
belongings winter will not want to see.

AUTOBIOGRAPHY

Say what you like I know
this pebble is part of a mountain
ground to bits by ice years
smoothed by water
buffed by wind
cleansed of memory
beyond all else learning
how to lie still

SNOW

The angels have voted
whether to admit me;

destroyed ballots fall
by thousand thousand,

each one to my musing marked
X yes   X no.

Through this feathered silence
no call has come;

I must of a truth conclude
the motion was defeated.

EASTER

So far out of time the listeners
stand, far out of memory
the tellings they once heard,
beyond restoring the lines
lost in erosion of faces,
response of all but faded eyes.

A swirl of girls guising
all secrets they know,
all tales they will not tell
for fear of spirits
writhing the soft sea air.

Meet the ships gently
swelling off shore, new listeners
hungering for narrative;
smother their speech with warmth
of lips like the sea's lips
lapping the receptive sand.

God or turbulent soul,
whoever you are, listening,
be told no new redemption
appears, turmoil, resolution.
Laughter mollifies the ancient
curse. There is no reason not
to rest, to stand still.

SCENE II

He: I come bearing a priceless present.

She: Priceless? By what currency, pray?

He: Priceless and in the present. I couldn't bear
to spend you in the past. Even garbed in a cloak
of forgetfulness you wouldn't crumble. You'd stick
like an unsuspected stone in my vitals, ready to spew
certain moments after I had lapsed into unconsciousness.

She: You place me in precarious balance. I'd rather
take my chance as lodged somewhere in your heart
than as a hidden menace ready to be discharged.
The heart can forget, I'd say, with less strain
than what you circumspectly refer to as the
vitals. Do I strike you as excrement?

He: That you strike me is well put. I had in mind the
pain of you. I merely exposed as simile
the sharpest pain I could think of.

She: After all this shunted talk, may I ask
what this present of yours is?

He: I'd say it was myself, save that I'm anything
but priceless. I bring a sort of seal
of an attachment referred to, for want of more
explicit clarification, as love. Do I make myself clear?

She: Crystally so. To put it plainly,
I think I could kiss you.

He: There's a dear girl. Shall we slip off
somewhere where the prying eye blunts against
the brick wall of understanding?

She: Sharp and blunt — quite a nice collative.
Yes, let's.

Exeunt

ANOTHER GROUNDHOG

It was a dead animal
to me; nothing more.
I had seen similar display
times uncounted. A natural end
to animals, I reflected
as I turned away.

Found it fastening on the mind.
Returned, drawn to further visits
as though some thread of reasoning
urged my steps.
In the progress of decay,
in course teeth bared.
I could scarce mistake the grin
as I turned away.

I CAME TOO LATE

Singer, I came too late to
your singing. You had your say
and were gone. I heard only echoes
of your once high phrasing, your words
fading now through a forest
of dying trees. Whispers in branches
accuse me in leafless syllables
of my tardy appearing. I did not sense
time passing. I was not aware
of birds gathering in flocks
for taking wing against the onset
of winter. Would I had been here.
Messages directed on the wind
die in their delivering if no ear
linger to listen, if no voice
rise in reply. You are absent
now, and will not come again. My words
do not know where to follow.
Breezes darken, colours cool,
your praises are not sung. I own only
this sense of having lost your offerings
before they were found.

SOUND AN ALARM

He is here to set the place
on fire; man with taper
stealing house to house,
peering in at windows,
looking for streets with the most
litter. Shall I stamp him out,
draw bead through upstair
window, alert
neighbours? Shall we throw
blizzard of bottles, fling
acids, have done with violence?
Or, simply get to bed,
sleep off our dream verities,
wake sensitized?
Sleep, deathly sleep,
most competent quieter.

MY BUTTERFLY

The butterfly on my thigh
was a lark, you might say,
she avowed. Don't let it move you
to speculation. I had long had
a fascination for tattooing;
morbid, if you like, or simply
childish, as you may choose.
I can see a curtain
lowering over your eyes like
the last motion of a stage-play,
the moment when what it all comes to
grips the senses. Tragic,
farcical, it is roughly the same.
Perhaps some future's glow may be tempered
by the frailest distraction,
glimpse of a summer country
misted by autumn apprehension.
You have to expect these things, always.
I see no necessity to assign
reason or charge to simple fact.
Accept it. I cannot hold to account
my butterfly.

SAINT LEONARD

Pray to St. Leonard for a fair wind.
My sail is set towards you;
my tiller's grip tightens. In the mind's distance
I see your dainty shore feet
pacing out your impatience. They tread
sands that are eternal; sands
that have endured unnumbered watchings,
uncounted tellings of the same story.
Tumbling waves
will show my disappearance, my appearing,
throw me at last against your strand,
into your waiting arms. They will sing
the sadness of a moment's bliss, a moment
dissolving into time.
      St. Leonard,
your breeze is a sorrow's drift, yet
be thanked, good spirit, for your tremulous
trial of one more spell, another knocking
softly upon the unanswered gate.

VERMEER: THE MILKMAID

The very milkstream
moves; the figure full of life;
of fine intent; concentration;
a necessary loneliness;
the miracle of light and shadow.

Did she herself move
she could be no livelier.
Did the light fail
she would shelve her pipkin
and be gone.

SEVEN-PETALLED FLOWER

Seven hands outspread,
perfect in seven times' outreaching,
drawn from earth by a parent sun.
What shall I name you?

Envy the sun opening you
morning by morning, envy
insects mounting you, withdrawing
sustenance, savouring your
scent and perfumed air;
vandals winging you away.

You are votive flickerings
from seven golden candlesticks;
holy ministrations in
a temple laid with precious stones.
Trust not mind to contain you.

The name stands unspoken.
The heart shrinks from its voicing.
The heart hears a passing-bell,
the late summer hours
of your appointed withering.
I am undone
in your own death's undoing.

THE MUSHROOM MAN

She came, the warmth of an autumn afternoon,
all scarlets and enticements. Stirred to her touch
grape clusters, purpled and dust-bloomed.
The lovers sighed in the soft wind,
the rising scales, the pricking senses singing,
the lips formed into ovals to receive
tongued messages from the moaning blood.
The mushroom man wrapped his arms about the sun,
making his own love motions. Winter came
without warning, all howl and driving ice needles,
frost blankets thrown over pallets where anon
love writhed in serpent twinings. (A past word
intrudes on liquid phrases.) Overnight
the graceless blooming.
                        Why did you walk
up and down those avenues, pacing boundaries
of your new discovered kingdoms?
Scarlet is celebration. I should choose rather
ruby, the saturate, the tincture of blood.

SLEEP-OUT

Wild men, I had not dreamed
your treading of these dark woods
would overtake me. What sense is
here envigoured? What attraction,
insect or animal, the call
of the night bird, the suggestive
whisper in the leaves, branch breath
that is not wind, the slightest stir
in conifer or gilead, the word
too still to be pronounced. Wild men,
I feel your mute surrounding. I can
touch, almost, your bending above me.
If you must work your will, it will
not wait the sunthrust of tomorrow's
bursting. Under these stars, pricked
through the dome of black, peeped upon
by heavenly quisitors, I suffer you
without want, without desire, without
your urgency's acceptance. I am here.
I know what tumults wait. I feel
the pressure of your breath about me,
wild, wild men.

NUDE WEARING HAT

Paint me like this or
not at all. All nudes are
alike. I have no novel feature.
If I'm to attract attention
it will have to be by
adornment superimposed.
Change the style if you will
as skill and wit dictate.
Erect feather,
furry aperture, brim
cocked at suggestive slant.
Surely someone will bring
to my brushstroke viewing
a modicum of imagination.

CRITIQUES

They say rude things about
the creatives. They know for certain
not only how it should have been
done, but the essential what.
They put them right back in
their places. Stay away from
this bare mountain, that
affirmation of incompetence,
and how to keep a fugue subject
waiting while you digress,
perhaps forget to answer
altogether. This was left
for his maturity, and is still
waiting.   Audiences perversely
take things to their hearts and
continue to applaud. Don't tell us
what to enjoy. We don't know
either, but we know when something
brings us up cheering. For whom was it
written anyway?

MIST OVER DUBLIN

Mr. Joyce whose sentences
seldom want to stop whose words
drop from skies like it was raining
frogs plop spatter croak
wishes to leave me swimming
in upper air of unsalted sea
seized upon by
claw and octo-tentacle
feel never again to fall
amphibian or meteor crash
where up where down
home here home there
care why care ever
pyrotechnics exploding
wink once wink when
to my shootstar stuttering

STITCHER'S MOON

> *thimbly click*
> *thimble toss and mumbly peg*
> *and the game scarce half over*

I thought how silly, drinking coffee from thimbles,
touching the lips to a stipple of black scald,
ten to the fluid ounce or my judgement's awry about
thimbles, until, listen to this now, until
having one by one nodded heads in agreement,
their spokesman, like a needle with two eyes, turning
one of them on me (not both, now) asked,
point to the blank, will you sup with us?
                                                                                   Yes,
with my thanks to you and your close company.
                                                                                                         Here;
and handed me a draught in fingers as delicate
as befit so intricate a ministration. I descried
the rim of gold lining showing above the portion,
thin swirl of a vapour so potent it could carry
aroma of the fresh grinding. Thankful I found it,
the silver surface chased to ease my bungling
grasp, when to be sure little in like of handle
could have steadied a facility so small, a sense
so depleted of the graces as was mine at that moment.

We drank a toast, too, though none that I recall
was proposed, despite drifting impressions that
I was myself its subject, reason enough for lingering

a stitch in time; but because no thimbles rose
to my focus, I joined in give-you whatever presence
their silence implied. And we tapped a rhythm out,
point to sharp point, for words not articulated
but none the less meet for the singing; it was

> *thimbly click*
> *thimble toss and mumbly peg*
> *and the game scarce half over*

Foolhardy, you think, accepting the face value
of an unsampled cup so far out of circumstance?
You put a thought in my head, one that goes crying
old clothes to mend, old clothes to mend, and carries
savour of what can never be again, its genesis
withheld. They meet in garrets in the fourteenth
moon, between a year and a year, a time not noted
on any calendar's contriving, is all they told me,
and you must come again; but why, indeed how,
I was not able to discover, nor have since been.
Yet beyond this season's time I can never sleep
faint soundly now, can never stop my ears
entirely to the beat of

> *thimbly click*
> *thimble toss and mumbly peg*
> *and the game scarce half over*

PRIERE ZOOLOGIQUE

In the eye of the elephant
I stand of so small account
as merely to magnify
inadequacies of peck or bushel
I bring trembling to offer to
his tusked gods.
                      (*peanuts peanuts customers*
                      please use shopping baskets)

What gods for elephants?
I hear a thunder as of trunks
thrashing mountain peaks,
belabouring the gates of temples.
                      (*please use the shopping baskets*)

On my knees, you pachydermal deities,
torn like the earth-vine,
I implore indulgence of elephants
for my shelled and petty crimes,
my skinbrown misdemeanors.
Do not answer me; accept
my sacrifice, let me work out
my circus of salvation
                      (*peanuts shopping baskets*)
with many roasted oblations. Receive
my whirl of carousel petitions
unrehearsed as the laughter of children.
Cool the soul in your breezes,
huge fans, gentle thermal ears.

THE GONDOLIERS

They have slept late. They rise
with never a memory one dares
repeat. Secrets of the confessional
are not more closely kept.
Love is a passing thing;
sacred for all that. They know
nothing to be exchanged over
their simple meal. A look here,
there a knowing nod; a word
never. What rare exchanges,
spoken or fleshed, let the water
whisper in a new sun's wrinkling;
let the night birds, nested, mutter
beneath their blanket, the protective
light of day. Our charges
rose at last and left us
strangers still, not a glance
exchanged, not a drawn breath's
injunction. Look to look
is all we need this grey repentant
morning. We have seen. We know.
Love is a passing thing.

A NEW COMMANDMENT

His crouch is grotesque; not prone, not hands and knees. A painful stance. The test by bitter water has backfired. The woman with the lash stands over him while he licks clean the temple floor. The law and the prophets are in shambles; the holy songs wrenched beyond plainchants. Selah: instruments strike up, voices be silent. Sheath your swords; the Phillistines are toy soldiers. It is too late. Clutch as you may, you will never tear from your throat the strangling and the streaming hair.

SET UPON BY DOGS

They are shadows only;
they cannot hurt you.
Only the razor fangs
are real.

The fangs are of thought
only. Only the rending,
the torn flesh itself,
is real.

The blood is in fancy
only. The unstaunched flow,
the rhythmic gushing, alone
is real.

The unlet draining away is not
so. Only the spreading stain,
shirt-front, sleeve, soaked
undergarment, is real.

Distant bayings in retreat
are imagined. Only this death,
this dearth, the mind emptied
of survivings, endures.

THE HIGH SEAS

I am a keel encrusted
with crustacean swarm

salt tides to suppress
unacceptable scents

dry dock to
cleanse and restore

to scrape and
fashion new

O but the high seas
romp and tumble

mouth for mouth
gasping and gaping

sing in chorus
ply every rhythm

every dissonance every
unrelated key

SPIDERS

no explaining
that boy
a pocketful of
dead spiders

a hank
smelling of
among possibilities
girl's hair

torn out of a
rice-grain bible
the gospel according
to St. John

REVOLUTION

I am back from the park
where I saw
expanses of green
muted cinder paths
shrubberies
birds in sunlight
and the world describing
one profitable revolution
cross-leg on a bench a citizen
reading a book

LITTLE MOUSE

Little mouse behind
my wainscot, be still
of your stirring.

It is Christmas Eve;
nativity is silence before
the first cry.

There are dusty stairs,
old attics, waiting
for silence to fall,

for starlight to shed
its blaze down
the quiet way.

Mouse in my wainscot,
you are gnawing a little hole
in my heart.

NIGHT VISIT

My chimney shudders. Soot flecks
flake the hearth. Down comes
my childhood, snow-bearded,
my greedy wishes sacked. I sleep
the sleep of the guilty, one dog's eye
open behind a camouflage of lashes.
Russet-cheeked, an old courier
selects my particulars, arranges them
with a random gesture, downs
my stale cookie, my mug of milk
long since congealed, leaps,
is gone. I think I hear
a sigh — a chimney, perhaps,
settling back to its star-watching.

'LO, HOW A ROSE'

Rose of prophecy, Rose
of the centuries' foretelling,
in the spring of our redemption
bid your bud swell, your fragrance
filter through our tainted air.
O Garden spirit,
discover our walkways,
answer our hunger with
your promise of refreshment;
send us rains, send us
warmth of your sun's rising,
your light's radiance;
suffer us not to fall again
sterile into darkness,
into the chill inhabiting
of our wintry night.

NATIVITY

They waited in the fields,
night and winter
throbbing at their ears,
eyes scanning the darkness
for prowling shapes
reflected in the firelight.

The tiding words
pierced the air like trumpets
sounding. How could they not
fulfil the quest, explore
that disturbance of history, the
upsetting of this quiet?

They insisted there were angels
singing hosannahs
that jewelled night, startling
the drowsing sheep.

Peace and a sword
dropped from the sky as one,
shocked the simple shepherds
fastfooting it to Bethlehem.

FEAST OF THE TRANSFIGURATION

Never morning lit
with such glory;
mountain shaken
to such wonder.

Never past and present
hopes so mingled;
figure of humanity
so transformed.

Three minions slowly
downhill to dusty
roads. Is there
glory still to come,
or have they seen an end
of vision, promise?

EMMAUS

The road would never be the same
since those footsteps. Speech itself
was in their prints. They were meant
to stay. The waning of light,
the spent sun's circuit,
brings on refreshment, rest,
unexpected explicatory. Had they parted
as he made as though, the prophets
would not have spoken; nor the bread,
set out and broken, become instant revelation.
Abide with us.
Give us this bread.